I0081917

DEDICATION

This book is dedicated to God who has a plan for me and orders my steps. I live knowing that:

The Lord is my shepherd; I shall not want. He maketh me to lie down in green pastures: He leadeth me beside the still waters. He restoreth my soul: he leadeth me in the paths of righteousness for his name's sake. Yea, though I walk through the valley of the shadow of death, I will fear no evil: for thou art with me; thy rod and thy staff they comfort me. Thou preparest a table before me in the presence of mine enemies: thou anointest my head with oil; my cup runneth over. Surely goodness and mercy shall follow me all the days of my life: and I will dwell in the house of the Lord for ever. Psalm 23

ISBN: **0692829776**

ISBN-13: **978-0692829776 (Amazon)**

TABLE OF CONTENTS

Introduction: Discover You   1

Chapter 1: Get Clear – Clarity of Purpose   3

Chapter 2: Create Your "On Purpose" Strategic Plan   19

Chapter 3: Connecting with Purpose   29

Chapter 4: Communicating Your Brand   37

Chapter 5: Capitalize on Opportunities   45

Summary   49

Goals & Tasks Form   51

Acknowledgements

I acknowledge all those who have planted seeds in me and nourished me throughout my life to learn, live and lead with all of the knowledge and experiences gained from family, friends, co-workers, business associates, and inspirational guides.

INTRODUCTION – DISCOVER YOU!

You are an IMPOSTER and it's time to get real and recognize who you truly are! Throughout your life you have been an impersonator, a fake, a pretender when living your life. You are impersonating the life of others, the direction of others, or defined by others. You choose dreaming about a life you saw on TV. You pretend you are in control of your life yet you are so out of control. You fake happiness, joy, laughter, and success. You have been playing different roles depending on the situation and circumstances. How is that working for you! For me, it wasn't working. I felt powerless to be me. The real me. The authentic me! How about you? You now can get your power back to live your life authentically. I have been liberated and want you to feel it as well.

STOP putting a shade over your light playing small when you have the power within you to have a much greater impact on your life and the lives of others. It has become imperative in our global society that we expand our thinking, competitive edge, and our lifestyles from a simple local to global perspective. Sometimes life and environmental circumstances make it "seem" impossible to achieve personal and business aspirations. However, more often, we simply don't organize ourselves to turn our aspirations into reality - and then "wake up" and find that life and our competitors have passed us. By taking this journey of self-discovery igniting the fire within you, you will discover your authentic self and set in motion wisdom choices to affect the change in you to be liberated to live!

What's the caveat? You MUST do the work! No one can do it for you to get the results you really want. You have put the work in for everyone else – family, job, church – but not paid enough attention on you and what you want, why, and what you are willing to do to achieve it. Ignite the Fire Within Through Self-Discovery will 1) help you gain clarity through discovery of your innate gifts; 2) organize yourself by creating a strategic plan of action to lead you to success as you define it; 3) recognize and eliminate your mind viruses (negative thinking) that block your success along with those that will lead to your success; 4) and exploit your talents highest potential through global thinking and actions. This program is a holistic approach resulting in a balanced, authentic, and successful overall lifestyle. Ignite Within's Self-Discovery program will provide you with the information, motivation, support, and accountability required to authentically live your life on purpose, bring energy and joy into all that you do.

What are some key benefits from doing the work?

- Thought-provoking and insightful perspective into YOU – Don't Be Scared!
- Expanded thinking and actions from a global perspective – Confirmed: The World is Flat!
- Clarity on where you are, where you want to be and why – Clarity, Clarity, and yes Clarity
- Move from awareness to attention to intention to action - Focus!
- Get comfortable with the certainty of uncertainty – Exhale!

Our 5 C-step methodology leading to your authenticity and success is:

Step 1: *Clarity through self-discovery*

Step 2: *Create reality of your purpose through strategic planning*

Step 3: *Connecting with Purpose*

Step 4: *Communicate locally, regionally, and globally with impact?*

Step 5: *Capitalize on the key opportunities and Wrap Up*

As you prepare to go on this journey of self-discovery, set your intention, be present with yourself to learn, live and lead with the messages and knowledge received.

Invest in YOU! YOU MATTER!

Chapter 1: Get Clear – Clarity of Purpose

According to Brian Tracey in The Law of Clarity, "The three keys to high achievement, success, and happiness are, Clarity, Clarity, and yes, Clarity about your goals. Your success in life will be largely determined by how clear you are about what it is you want." - your must haves. Lack of clarity is more responsible for frustration and underachievement than any other single factor. Have you ever wondered how you can become more satisfied in life - how you can enjoy life more than ever? Only by discovering your innate strengths, developing and exploiting them to their highest degree can you ever fully realize the greatest amount of satisfaction and enjoyment in everything you do. At various stages of our life, we find ourselves in moments of transition. If you are seeking answers to find purpose, direction, clarity, and focus having a better state of mind, improved relationships, and life contributions, you are in the right place!

You are on your way to GETTING CLEAR about your life, business, and career. The intention behind this program is to help you discover and get clarity on your authentic self, overcome mind viruses and stress, improve on making right decisions resulting in momentum for success as you have defined it for yourself and family. Set your intention to be successfully led through this insightful process to get the answers you've longed to know to plan your future to reach your next level of success.

Within this module on Clarity, you will go through five reflections and actions: 1) Strategic Life Map; 2) Clarity Statement 3) Mind Viruses; 4) Visualization; and 5) Your Big Why's

1. Strategic Life Map. As Stephen Covey said "I am not a product of my circumstances. I am a product of my decisions."

Understanding where you are today is a critical step in getting clarity on where you are now. Reflection on your key life areas will help you to understand what you've been paying attention to and in what areas you need to shift your attention to have a well-balanced life. The Ignite Your Life – Strategic Life Map gives you reflection on **the seven key areas of your life** - Health, Family and Friends, Love, Purpose, Finances, Passions, and Spirituality. With this reflection, you must be specific, honest, and aspirational as you assess and understand your goals in these areas. The intention is not for you to stress about this but to be honest and consider this a journey of understanding and transformation.

For each of the seven life areas, I want you to do three things. One to reflect on where you've been, are and want to go. Two to rank where you are currently from 1-5 with one being the lowest and five the highest. And three-set three goals or habits that would improve each area.

Health: Are you optimizing your physical and emotional health and well-being. Are you energetic, motivated with a strong mental and physical stamina? Reflect on the past, present, and future, rank where you are now, set three goals.

Reflection: _____

_____

_____

_____

_____

_____

Rank (1-5) _____

Goals/Habits

1) _____

_____

2) _____

_____

3) _____

_____

Family and Friends: Can you say I am authentic in my relationships with family and friends and I am surrounded by positive people. I am very connected, present, and bring positive energy into their lives.

Reflection: _____

_____

_____

_____

_____

_____

Rank (1-5) _____

Goals/Habits

1) _____

_____

2) _____

_____

3) _____

_____

Love: Do you feel compassion and love for all people and those you interact with. Can you say, with my significant other, my connection is deep, trusting, loving, appreciative, and spirit filled. I love my partner and demonstrate patience, respect, and attention. If you don't have a significant other, do you live your life in an open, loving, and connected way? Are you patient and peace-filled with positive expectation for this partnership?

Reflection: _____

_____

_____

_____

_____

_____

_____

Rank (1-5) _____

Goals/Habits

1) _____

_____

2) _____

_____

3) _____

_____

Purpose: Can you say - I have clarity on my purpose in life? I am energized and fulfilled by the work I do and my contribution to humanity which adds "real" value to the world. It is a true reflection of the best me which helps me to enjoy and experience the lifestyle I want.

Reflection: _____

_____

_____

_____

_____

Rank (1-5) _____

Goals/Habits
1) _____

_____

2) _____

_____

3) _____

_____

Finances: I am in a good and comfortable place with my finances. I am living the lifestyle I want today and the future. I am able to be supportive of those requiring my financial support.

Reflection: _____

_____

_____

_____

_____

_____

Rank (1-5) _____

Goals/Habits
1) _____

_____

2) _____

_____

3) _____

_____

Passions: I take the time to enjoy those things that I am passionate about beyond work and career.

Reflection: _____

_____

_____

_____

_____

Rank (1-5) _____

Goals/Habits

1) _____

_____

2) _____

_____

3) _____

_____

Spirituality: I am connected to a source higher than myself, living in the present moment. My actions are aligned and guided by my beliefs, faith, and values which are at the forefront of all my decisions and day to day actions.

Reflection: _____

_____

_____

_____

_____

_____

Rank (1-5) _____

Goals/Habits

1) _____

_____

2) _____

_____

3) _____

_____

I am going to congratulate you in advance for completing Step 1. I can do that because you set your intention!! Don't let yourself down – Do this and begin your journey of transformation!

The Mindset of LIMITATION

Congratulations on completing the process to reflect on the seven key areas of your life. Have you realized that you have some work to do as you neglected particular areas of your life over others? Even if you're doing well, you have goals that will accelerate you further to improve your overall life. To ensure you stay motivated on this journey of self-discovery, I want to share with you the five things that contribute to not achieving success as you've defined it in your life areas. Don't allow this to happen! Be intentional!

- Limited attention and focus you give – attention will change the outcome in your life!
- Limited emotional connection and commitment – engage with your heart!
- Limited routine and habitual action – refer at least monthly to re-assess!
- Limited desire to improve – determine these life areas are "must haves"!
- Limited control or influence, victim versus victor – be the victor!

Don't be LIMITED be LIMITLESS on your journey through life! Based on your reflection and completing your Strategic Life Map, take action on two things:

Select the three top areas of focus which you will embrace to ignite the power within you

_____

_____

_____

Select four key goals that you want to focus and work on throughout this program (these will be leveraged further during module #2 strategic planning process).

_____

_____

_____

_____

Developing Your Clarity Statement
What's Your Purpose, Passion, Values, Impact, and Outcome?

"Strive not to be a success, but rather to be of value!" – Albert Einstein

Uncovering who you are at your core will get you clarity on your purpose, gifts, passion, impact, values, and personal outcomes. This inward exercise will deliver to you your strategic Clarity Statement which you will use as the basis to align your strategic plan and actions. It is important to do this work first. Otherwise, your actions will equate to throwing spaghetti against the wall to see what sticks. And we wonder why the frustration, no growth, and achievement at a pace and level that we know we want. You will complete the below five sections of your Clarity Statement and at the end create your full Statement. Reflect on it – how does it make you feel, excited, ready to go or nervous, anxious. Keep reflecting and changing if need be until reading it gets you excited from within.

The first section is about purpose. So, what makes the gifts given to you by God you? What do you love to do most and well! It is also important to understand how you are using or not using these gifts today. What do I mean by the traits of someone's gifts? It's not about a job, i.e., electrician, teacher or skill set, i.e., computer, math, typing, or photography. It's more about what are the outcomes of using your gifts. I have been given the gift of coaching, speaking, and teaching. I use them to bring out the potential in others, to advance ideas and to make people feel good about themselves. Could yours be to –analyze information, build things, build relationships, create or design things, crunch numbers, help others? Are you getting my point? Name as many as you can, reflect on them to determine which get you "most" excited, that you feel great about doing. My spirit lights up, and I feel within me excited when I see the transformation in people I've helped. Ask if the traits you've realized are showing up for you currently as you go through your life, business and career? Why or why not? Once you know this, you then need to understand what gets you most excited and proud, that show up or don't show up in your daily life. Are any of them tough for you to do? At this point, don't worry about can you make money or how would you apply these traits. You are conducting a brainstorming and reflective exercise that will help you to understand more clearly the outcome of using your gifts.

Why do you use your gifts? My purpose for using my gifts is to:_____

_____
(Fxample: bring out the potential in others)

The second section is your passion. What is your passion? I am passionate about giving guidance and direction. It all goes back to my purpose to bring out the potential in others. What about you? Is it entertainment, politics, cultural, business, or social? When you think about it, does it make you smile? Do you feel good inside? If you feel any anxieties, consider is this a passion or something you do because someone told you it's the right thing for you to do or something someone else is doing and they are successful. Be true, honest with yourself on what brings you joy through the good, bad, and ugly.

List your top three passions without judgment initially. Then reflect on them and feel what is resonating and which one gets you most excited and peace filled. Once you have that, complete the second part of your clarity statement. I have a passion for: _____

_____
(Example: giving guidance and direction)

The third section is who you will impact. Whatever you do in your life, business or career it "must" have a positive impact on someone other than yourself. Otherwise, what's the point? Where's the joy in only satisfying yourself? Based on the purpose and passions you've identified, who does it impact? For me, it's my clients-women and girls and thereby the community because they will be more confident and empowered, their standard of living will rise bringing value to their families who will bring value to communities.

So, who are you impacting? Name your top three and prioritize. Complete this sentence: My purpose will have an impact on: _____

_____
(Example: my clients; women and girls and thereby, the community)

The fourth section is about your must keep values throughout the journey. Regardless of the obstacles, struggle, pains that may come you remember the meaning and importance of these values. What are the three essential qualities that you value? I value integrity, excellence, honesty. Prioritize - Complete this sentence – I value _____

_____
(Example: integrity)

The last section of your clarity statement is understanding what you will get out of doing all of this – Your Outcome. We should have a selfish perspective as well – it's ok!! Remember you are expending your energy! What return do you want to get? Complete this sentence – My outcome will be to _____

_____
(Example: be valued, loved, and secure)

CLARITY STATEMENT
Consolidate the five parts of the clarity statement previously completed to get the whole statement. Read it out loud, reflect on it. How does it make you feel? Are you peace filled, excited or do you have some anxieties? Don't worry about how you will get there yet. If it doesn't feel right, reflect again on each part to ensure you are comfortable. This clarity statement will be your guide as you journey through life. Everything thing you do needs to align with your clarity statement.

My Example Clarity Statement:
I want to use my gifts for the purpose of bringing out the potential in others allowing my passion for giving guidance and direction to create an impact on women and girls. My values of integrity and excellence and my personal outcome of being valued, loved, and secure will be embedded in the heart all of my actions.

Every step I take both personally and professionally I ensure aligns with my Clarity Statement. My Clarity Statement helps me to focus, be decisive, and live on purpose.

Now, what is your Clarity Statement?

"I want to use my gifts for the purpose of _____

_____

allowing my passion for _____

_____

to create an impact on _____

_____

My values of _____

_____

and my personal outcome of being _____

_____

will be embedded in the heart of all of my actions."

Four Must-Do Directives to Be Present in Your Life

"With mindfulness, you can establish yourself in the present in order to touch the wonders of life that are available in that moment" – Thich Nhat Hanh

Let's talk about what you need to do to be mindful or present with your emotional, mental, physical and environmental experiences. It is vital to your self-discovery and transformation. The four must do directives to be present in your life is to be aware, pay attention, set the intention, and act!

Being aware is the key to change! If you don't know, you can do nothing! Nothing in a proactive way. You are vulnerable to whatever comes your way. I want you to take your power back and be in a state of awareness as much as possible.

Your current status in life, business, and career is where your attention has lied. That's difficult to accept I know. But we have to stop blaming other people, circumstances, and situations. Your focus or attention has to be on YOU only and only YOU! Yes, I know – you feel you have to focus on everyone else but you. Not true. Your BEST you will infect those around you. Pay attention to what you are thinking, feeling, and doing. And determine is it in the right place.

Setting your intention ignites the fire within you! You must be deliberate and purposeful to set your mindset that a change in course is a must do. You can't be weak about this. There is power in the first person words I AM and what comes after those words. The statement I am doing the work is a stronger statement than I am trying to do it. The latter does not leave one confident in you. Be careful, courageous, and intentional when you speak.

No action, no results! You can be aware, pay attention, and set a bold intention. But if you don't set it in play or take action, nothing will change – you cannot transform. For example, I am aware that I need to lose weight for healthy aging. I am paying attention to it because it is always on my mind – at the grocery store, restaurant, or when I may be stiff when I get out of bed. I have set the intention so many times that I am going to lose the weight and have even taken "action" – got a room full of exercise equipment. But I'm talking about the for real – real!! The "wisdom" choice of what I must do versus try to do! I've lost 30 lbs. WHAT IS YOUR MUST DO ACTION?

Mind Viruses; Five Beliefs to Propel You Forward or Hold You Back:

"Everything you've ever wanted is on the other side of fear" – George Addair

As we continue with Step 6 in getting Clarity of Purpose - What does it mean to have fear or be afraid? What does it feel like to be fearful?   How can it impact you and others? Fear can dominate your attention and becomes your focus. Your results reflect your focus. Before I talk about the mind virus which are beliefs that can propel you forward or hold you back, let's discuss what the heck is a mind virus and how does it impact you – "and others close to you." A mind virus is a thought, belief, or attitude in your mind that can spread. I know you thought it only impacts you but not so! Just like a computer or flu virus, if you connect your infected computer to another computer or sneeze on someone else, whatever you touched, in many times the smallest way, will infect them also. So does how you think and the attention, intention, and actions you put behind it. I know you've been affected either by someone's negative or positive energy.

I have been feeling great and talked to someone who was negative and felt my energy change, or I find myself agreeing. I'm not the only one now! So who are you infecting right now and how are you poisoning them – your significant other, children, friends, other family, co-workers, bosses, clients, etc.   It subtly influences your behavior and just keeps spreading.

Who you are has been formed throughout your life based on what you believed was possible. How you see yourself and how you think others see you, dominates your thinking (which is what you are paying attention to) on your capability and readiness to reach new heights. You must change your mind viruses to affect the positive change and growth you seek. I have a t-shirt that says – Don't Believe Everything You Think! I add to that – Believe Everything You Feel because it's telling you something! If its feelings of anxiety – anger, sadness, frustration, judging, etc. you need to be "aware," pay "attention," set your "intention," and "act"! If its feelings of peace, love, joy, happiness, etc., do the same. You want to know what makes you feel good and get more of it!

You want to use a new set of thinking habits to enhance your life to be all you were meant to be. Every person you know also live with their mind viruses. You can be the example. Let's review and reflect on how the below five beliefs can be a negative or positive influence on your life, business, or career. The point is to ensure your awareness of the excuses you use for behaving in ways that don't help you achieve the level of health, overall well-being, and success you deserve!

How are they showing up for you? You may be experiencing others, add as appropriate. Remember, these can propel you forward or hold you back! Understand these five beliefs to ensure they are propelling you forward. I encourage you to reflect on these and write down your cure! Remember: "*The key to success is to focus our conscious mind on things we desire not things we fear.*" — Brian Tracy

Worthiness: Do you feel worthy of success, love, joy, abundance, peace? Why or Why not? If not, you are limiting your potential. If yes, then the energy of attraction will work to get you what you need to achieve it. What are you worthy of? _____

_____

_____

_____

_____

Readiness: Do you fear failure if you make your next move? Timing not right. Don't have enough knowledge, skill, talent, or ability. Do you freeze or move forward? Is I can't or I can in your vocabulary? Are you listening to someone else saying you're not ready or it will never work? Fear will keep you where you are. Will you work until you figure it out or quit? Do you need all the answers? Would you be happier if you made the move if there were no risks? (No such thing) You can mitigate your risks. _____

_____

_____

_____

Desire: Do you have the desire to do what it takes - learn new things, go for new opportunities and to receive constructive feedback? Do you "want" to achieve success or be joyful in the midst? Do you want to learn or do you get defensive on the learning journey? Do you desire hearing and trying new ideas to grow. _____

_____

_____

_____

_____

Perseverance: Do you have a tendency to give up when the going gets tough? You struggle through difficulty, uncertainty, chaos, and rejection. Or is your mentality, "I'll keep trying until I achieve my dream even when it's hard." _____

_____

_____

_____

_____

Am I Enough: I have had to ask myself this question several times. Especially when I give, and give, and give some more and my giving is not recognized or more is still wanted. I've learned to sit with myself and once I get comfortable that I am doing what I should do, I release myself from the outcome of what others may think. Do you see yourself as a role model—for your kids, family, your neighbors, your employees, and your co-workers? Do you understand that people are paying attention to your energy and actions, and you want to be a positive role model or leader for others? Does that make you feel empowered or powerless?_____

_____

_____

_____

Understanding, reflecting, and determining whether you are "allowing" your mind viruses to propel you forward or hold you back is critical to discovering who you are, to know where you are, to know what you need to change, to ensure the fearless transformation toward success that you desire and define for you. Regarding these mind viruses, it doesn't matter the type of career or business, married or single, children no children – it is an equal opportunity virus and impacts all of us. The great thing is YOU have the power to determine its impact on your life and what you pass on to others. (By the way, it is up to the other person to be aware, pay attention, set the intention, and act on what they are receiving)

Your authentic self – the real you – the original you – your soul/spirt is not the negative thoughts that you allow yourself to pay attention to. I learned from my Pastor – Dr. King that when these negative thoughts invade our bodies, we have to supplement those thoughts with positive ones. For example, becoming a new business owner – I had a mind virus on readiness and worthiness. I didn't think I was ready to launch my business. I needed to do one more thing, dot the i, and cross the t. I had the fear that I could not be successful, even with my success in Corporate, that no one would pay me or show up for my workshop. I told my coach I wasn't ready, she said you're ready – press the launch button (to send out my announcement email). I said – The Lord is My Shephard I Shall Not Want and pressed the button and people have found me worthy to pay for my services and attend my events. I had to challenge my mind viruses in order to move forward. I'm glad I did – or I would not be with you in this moment! I encourage you to challenge the mind viruses that is holding you hostage!

Remember DON'T BELIEVE EVERYTHING YOU THINK!! BELIEVE EVERYTHING YOU FEEL!! Reflect and take action on your Mind Viruses.

Visualization - See Your Future

"Believe you can, and you are half way there." – Theodore Roosevelt

We discussed previously the importance of what you believe. It is critical that you can visualize what you want to achieve continually to strengthen your positive belief system. An excellent way to do that is through a vision board. A vision board is one of the most successful methods of identifying, clarifying and focusing either what it is you desire in life, business, and career. It's about seeing your future. There's no right or wrong way to do it. It's a means of attracting to you what you desire. Remember you've got to do the work we've discussed to ensure you "know" what you want and "desire" minimizing your fears. You will regularly visit the board as a way to bring your focus back to what you want.

Below are some simple steps to develop your vision board. Be sure to set aside three hours in your private space. Remember this is about what YOU want with NO bounds.

Step 1: Get your mind right! Visualization is about YOU and what you want. Don't think about how it will be achieved. The achievement plan comes later. You have no boundaries and no fear! Remember you are worthy of achieving the success you desire.

Step 2: Gather materials – poster board, tape, magazines that align with what you want or go online through Google, magazines, etc. You can also create a digital vision board using the same steps. There are several online tools at no cost. For my digital board, I used PicMonkey, but you can also use PicStitch (smartphone app for iPhone and Android), or Oprah, com's O Dream Board to help you build your online collection of inspiring images. I keep my bucket list vision board as the screen saver on my phone and tablet as a constant reminder.

Step 3: Gift yourself a half day in private spot to go through the process

Step 4: Start finding your images and words that make your soul sing and that resonates and aligns with your life, business, and career goals.

Step 5: Lay out your pictures, words, and letters whether physically or online. Look at them and "be" with it. How do you feel about what you've laid out? You want to be completely comfortable. If you're not, it is alright to change out images or rearrange them on the board. But don't change anything out of fear you can't achieve it. Remember you are boundless in this exercise. Visualization is not about how you will achieve it. That comes in later modules. You can put those of highest priority or shorter term on the top portion of the board if you like. Do whatever gives you comfort when looking at the board.

Step 6: Put the board in a place that you visit frequently. Take a picture of your board and make it your home screen on your computer or mobile device.

Know Your Big Whys – NEVER QUIT, Think About Why You Started!

Congratulations on completing the Self-Discovery - Clarity of Purpose Module. You've gone through completing your Strategic Life Map, Clarity Statement, understanding the importance of being present, identifying and resolving your Mind Viruses, and Visualization through your vision board. Let's wrap up and end with a Clarity of Purpose one pager of the main thoughts. The one pager will be a snapshot that you will review for this to stay top of mind as a reminder of your direction in life and what will drive your behavior to success as you have defined it!

You will start with your Clarity Statement. Remember everything aligns with this. My Clarity Statement is: **I want to use my gifts for the purpose of bringing out the potential in others allowing my passion for giving guidance and direction to create an impact on** women and girls. My values of integrity and excellence with my personal outcome of being valued, loved, and secure is embedded in the heart of all of my actions.

Your Clarity Statement is:

"I want to use my gifts for the purpose of _____

_____

allowing my passion for _____

_____

to create an impact on _____

_____

My values of _____

_____

and my personal outcome of being _____

_____

is at the heart of all of my actions."

What are your 3 Big Why's – Three words that drive you and keep you going and why it's important? Mine are to 1) God said so, 2) bringing value, and 3) makes me feel good
1)
2)
3)

What are the 3 words that guide your thoughts, actions, and personal life and why is it important to you? Mine are love, integrity, and authenticity
1)
2)
3)

What are the 3 words that guide and define how you will engage and treat others that you meet and know in your life and why is it important? You don't live on an island. Mine are authenticity, love, compassion
1)
2)
3)

What are the 3 words that demonstrate what has made you most successful with even greater success ahead and why is it important to you? Mine are value others, signature of excellence, persistence
1)

2)

3)

What are your good, bad, and empowering habits and what will you do about them?

Good Habits _____

_____

_____

_____

_____

_____

Bad Habits _____

_____

_____

_____

_____

Empowering Habits _____

_____

_____

_____

_____

_____

Congratulations on completing the first chapter of your journey towards Self-Discovery – Clarity of Purpose. If you did the work, you should be clear on where you are, want to be, and some of the work needed to do within yourself to ensure you reach your goals. You should feel excellent about your accomplishment of getting clear about YOU!! If not, reflect on why. Were you focused paying attention and setting the intention to act? Do the work. Continue to sit with yourself on what you have learned about you and massage the work you've done if you feel the need to – not out of fear! You should be getting to a better place of peace and fulfilment and excitement about your direction. The next phase of discovery now that you are clear is to set your strategic plan to focus on achievement.

I am excited for you on your journey of self-discovery! According to Vernon Howard, "An authentically strong-minded person does not need the approval of others any more than a lion needs the approval of sheep!" What a powerful statement! BE YOU, IT'S YOUR LIFE, YOUR CHOICE, and YOUR DECISION!

Chapter 2: Create Your "On Purpose" Strategic Plan

INTRODUCTION

Now that you received clarity and you are ignited through the Ignite the Fire Within Clarity of Purpose chapter, your next step is to take the concepts from this work and make them more real by creating your strategic plan for your life, business, and/or career. Strategic planning is critical to creating success of your short and long term direction and is the roadmap to ensure success. It takes foresight, understanding probabilities, and dealing with uncertainties in both your personal and external environments. Your strategy must maximize your strengths and minimize the strengths of your competition – locally, regionally, and globally. It will bridge the gap of "where you are" versus "where you want to be" and provide the necessary map on "how to get there". Go back to your Clarity Statement and ensure your plan is in alignment.

VISION STATEMENT

The first thing you must know when developing your strategic plan is knowing your Mission, Vision, and End State. Your goals should then align with strategic direction providing a means to accomplishment. Your Clarity Statement can be used to complete your mission statement. Remember my Clarity Statement: I want to use my gifts for the purpose of bringing out the potential in others allowing my passion for giving guidance and direction to create an impact on women and girls. My values of integrity and excellence with my personal outcome being valued, loved, and secure is at the heart of all my actions. My mission statement - Ignite Within's mission is to bring out the potential of women and girls through guidance and direction that gives them a global competitive advantage raising their standard of living with significant impact on their family and community.

Next is your vision statement. A vision statement identifies where you want or intend to be in future to best meet the needs of those you want to impact (from your clarity statement). It describes your dreams and aspirations for future. This will help you with practical decision making about your future as well as effective planning towards your purpose. It should describe how your future will be when your purpose/mission is achieved.

Ensure your statement includes the following attributes:

a.   It must be unambiguous.

b.   It must be clear.

c.   It must harmonize with your values.

d.   The dreams and aspirations must be rational/realistic.

e.   Vision statements should be shorter so that they are easier to memorize.

My vision statement is: *Ignite Within moves its global clients away from any fears to live their highest purpose and potential in life, business, and career thereby uplifting communities in which they serve.*

Write Your Vision Statement: _____

_____

_____

_____

_____

_____

Goals – Short, Long Term, and Focused

According to Abraham Lincoln, "a goal properly set is half-way reached". A goal is a desired future state or objective that you want to achieve. Goals specify in particular what must be done if you want to attain your purpose/mission and vision. Goals make it more prominent and concrete.

There are three mistakes made when setting goals:

1. Achievable goals are set. You must step outside your zone of knowing, comfort zone (like walking - fall, get up, fall, get up to then walk, expect failures. Is reward/inspiration bigger than the pain?

2. You set goals based on what is known (environmental, internal). There is a law of movement or vibration and a constant state of change with everything in the universe. Don't have all your emotional investment in the plan. Know that based on changes in the environment you may have to make modifications. What's the outcome vs goal vs the plan itself? Focus on the goal and outcome. Typically one lowers the goal to meet the plan. Where do I want to be and what do I want?

3. You require knowing exactly how to do it in order to meet the goal. The implication is if I don't know how, it can't be done. Other people ask us how we will do it and we ask ourselves in our mind. You can't look at the how based on current resources. You don't know how you will achieve your goal precisely. How many plans did the Wright brothers have before achieving success? They kept their eye on the goal – their vision – their purpose!

What are 7 important considerations in setting your goals?
• Be precise, measureable, and time targeted
• Focus on critical and significant issues and opportunities
• Be realistic yet challenging
• Consider the financial and non-financial
• Goals are based on the outcomes you want to achieve
• Align with your core values, what you want, the pain to avoid, and lifestyle
• Must make you "feel" excited

I have included a table at the end of the book that you can leverage providing you with the categories to consider when developing your goals. Take the time to note your goals. You can have goals set for the priority areas of your life, business or career, the key goals identified during your Strategic Life Map exercise, or all of the 7 key areas on your life map. Ensure your goals are aligned to your clarity statement and vision while remembering your big whys!

IMPORTANT – GOALS are there to INSPIRE YOU not to beat yourself with them. State your goals in the positive, i.e. "I want healthy aging" rather than "I want to lower my blood pressure." What you do to ensure healthy aging will encompass what you need to do to ensure manageable blood pressure, cholesterol, etc.

Below are the categories you need to consider, when setting your goals you can download the Goals template from ignitewithin.org that provides an example (On Purpose Goals template pg. 51-52).

• Key Life Area (from Strategic Life Map), Goal, Completion Date, Tasks Required to Complete the Goal, Return on Energy (Yes or No), Task Completion Date, Obstacles to Achieve Goal, Skill Gaps, Resources Needed, and Opportunities Identified

Remember to reflect on the 7 considerations in setting your goals above – focused on outcomes, aligned to your values, goal to big or too small, etc. This work is important and

will give you the focused direction you need to get the highest return on your energy and time.
Strengths, Weaknesses, Opportunities and Threat (SWOT) Analysis

A SWOT analysis is a framework for analyzing your strengths and weaknesses as well as the opportunities and threats that you face. This helps you focus on your strengths, minimize your weaknesses, and take the greatest possible advantage of opportunities available to you.

Businesses leverage a widely known technique to analyze their SWOT. It also perfectly applies personally helping you to reflect on how to best succeed as you have defined success. Begin to differentiate yourself from your peers and competitors by using the SWOT framework.

You are most likely to succeed in life if you use your gifts to their fullest extent leveraging your strengths and opportunities. However, problems will arise if you don't know what are your weaknesses and threats. You can mitigate your risks through planning to reduce the level of potential suffering through avoidance. When completing your analysis think about how the regional and global competitive environment impacts each area of your review.
Let's go deeper into each sector. After, you will complete your SWOT analysis which can be based on your life, business, or career.

When considering your **STRENGTHS** what differentiates you? Why would someone choose you over their other alternatives? Consider the below and think through others personal to you.

- access to influential resources
- how do others see you
- key accomplishments
- unique values

Some of my personal examples are my leadership experiences working and living in Africa, working in multiple industries and functions, success with start-up organizations, client advocacy, and interpersonal skills.

What are your **WEAKNESSES**? Be honest! Do you procrastinate or have negative habits? What about your education, skills, or qualifications needed? Where do you lack confidence, i.e., public speaking? Are you being outperformed in critical areas? I know

I have a skill gap with social media and understanding how to optimize it to promote my brand and drive opportunities. Because it is a vital part of my business and personal engagements, I invested in a boot camp to learn more and now outsourced the work to a social media strategist. Know your lane!

Also, importantly, look at your strengths, and ask yourself whether these open up any opportunities – and look at your weaknesses, and ask yourself whether you could open up opportunities by eliminating those deficiencies. Because of my experience and exposure in Africa, I leverage that in my conversations and creating an opportunity to work with women from Africa now in the US on transition strategies which is a weakness not in the people but the process.

What are the OPPORTUNITIES available to you? Think about new technologies, resources, impact of market trends, strategic influential connections, weaknesses of the competition, or problems that need to be solved. Where could some of your opportunities come from? Mine have come from networking events, educational classes, and conferences. By being engaged in those events with like-minded people, I was able to get clients, speaking engagements, and podcast and TV interviews. You must engage with others! Is there a new role or project that gives you the opportunity to learn new skills like public speaking or global relationships or promotion or clients? Look for business expansions. Think about what opportunities your strengths can bring.

Finally, let's consider those external THREATS that can be obstacles in achieving success. Some of the threats could be competition (Are you globally competitive?), job changing or company laying off workers, technology threatening your position, or the market demand changing. As a single woman, an external threat can be the imbalance of the ratio of eligible men to women. Can any of your weaknesses lead to threats? Look at the manufacturing industry now requiring more skilled labor due to technology. If you don't up your skills or relocate or position yourself for the next new wave, that weakness poses a threat to your success.

Performing this analysis will often provide critical information – it can point out what needs to be done and put problems into perspective. Included on the next page is a template that you can leverage to complete your overall SWOT analysis.

MY SWOT ANALYSIS

STRENGTHS	WEAKNESSES

OPPORTUNITIES	THREATS

MANAGE YOUR TIME

Do you procrastinate? Do you lack focus on your priorities that will yield the best results? Provided below are some essential techniques that will help you achieve greater success when executing your strategic plan by increasing your productivity to get it done. Whether in life, business, or career you must deliver high performance on the right things to be successful and to ensure a competitive advantage.

FOCUS ON WHERE YOU'RE INVESTING YOUR ENERGY: This requires that you concentrate your talents and abilities where they will yield the highest payoff to you at the moment. I saw a chart that asked if your energy was spent on tasks that would yield you $1, $10, $100 or $1000. It put into perspective how you're spending your energy and where you should be investing your energy if you are the leader of your life, business or career. The solid return on the energy you expend will not be on the $1 or $10 task. At a conference I attended, a speaker asked how much time the audience spent on performance, exposure, and image in the workplace. As women, we said 90% on performance. Well, men had more balance ensuring they were investing time on exposure and image while still performing. And we wonder why we, when we are working like a mule, are passed for opportunity. Reflect on how you are investing your energy and is it yielding the results you want. It is your personal productivity and is essential to success in your personal strategic planning.

Businesses are always looking for a means to increase their return on equity and investment ROE/ROI to yield the highest return on its investments. It is equally as important to understand and see a performance of the energy (ROE) you invest to execute on your goals and to review how you can increase your return. This is done by properly allocating your talent and abilities aligning to the specific needs of the situation in a way that achieves the highest rate of return on the energy (physical, emotional, and mental) you invest in achieving your success. You then focus and concentrate single-mindedly (multi-tasking is over-rated and can't be done) on that one task, which is the key to getting things done efficiently. It takes discipline and practice. Always ask yourself: Does this work align with my purpose and will it yield the highest return on the energy I expend?" The same applies across your life, business, and career. "Does my business, career, job, company, or current family situation align with my purpose and yield the highest return for me?"

FOCUS ON TOMORROW'S OPPORTUNITY: While you must reflect on the problems of yesterday establishing a plan to fix, it is imperative that you focus on the opportunities of tomorrow. You can increase your productivity by leveraging your strengths and energy and those of all your essential resources on your major opportunities where breakthroughs are possible. Stop being bogged down in the problem. Can you see the forest and the trees? What does tomorrow look like for you?

FOCUS ON RESULTS NOT PROBLEMS: Identify the key results you expect from you and those you serve. Go back to your big why from the clarity of purpose work. "Why am I doing what I am doing and what is the key result I want to accomplish? This becomes your investment of your time.   Remember you thought through your clarity of purpose, vision, and goals. We are working harder and longer hours with no end in site. It takes you away from family and chill time. Don't you want to increase your productivity to balance your time and life? Of course you do!! Focus on the right things and get it done in less time with better results.   Note up to six key result areas below:

IF NOT NOW, WHEN? You have to write down what you need to do, set deadlines for important goals and stick to them. Deadlines force you to work harder and more efficiently as the deadline approaches. A goal or an assignment without a time limit is practically useless. There's no sense of importance or motivation. How do you focus or close on something that never has to get done. What's the point? It is procrastination waiting to happen and is happening! Since we don't live on an island, everything you do involves other people. Commit to them your completion date. You will then find the motivation to make it happen on time. There is almost no better feeling that saying or checking off DONE or ACCOMPLISHED.

Still having trouble **CHUNK IT**: Just as you would never try to eat a whole loaf of salami at once, don't try to take on all of a task from the start. Sometimes the best way to stop procrastinating and complete a primary task is to take a small chunk and complete just that piece. When you select a small part of the task and then discipline yourself to do it and get it behind you, it will often give you the momentum you need to counter.

CHALLENGE YOUR FEAR FIRST: Do the task that causes you the most fear or anxiety. Often, it has to do with overcoming the fear of failure or rejection by someone else. In sales, it may be associated with prospecting. In leadership, it may be associated with disciplining or firing an employee. In relationships, this may have to do with confronting an unhappy personal situation. In every case, you will be more efficient if you deal first with whatever is causing you the greatest emotional distress or fear. Often this will break the blockage experienced in your work and free you up mentally and emotionally to get things done. Think about what are the consequences to not complete vs completing the task. Which fear is greater? Make a wisdom choice!

GET YOUR RHYTHM: You now know how to avoid procrastination - waiting until the very last minute to finish the presentation, study for that exam, file your taxes. Get into a comfortable rhythm and begin early enough doing one thing at a time. Remember multi-tasking when you think about it can't be done. Normally, we skip around (completing a presentation, stopping to answer a call or check email, or just gazing). Work steadily. I have found when I have my rhythm I end the day feeling more accomplished minimizing my anxiety. Set your priority for the day or week and get it done.

Congratulations on completing the Self-Discovery – Creating Your Strategic Plan chapter. Your confidence in you must be noticeably different. Are you walking and talking differently? How are you feeling right now knowing you have clarity of purpose and have a plan of action to achieve it? You should be feeling more at peace and joyful because you are getting your power back!! If you are feeling some anxiety, understand where that's coming from. What are your fears and why are you fearful? What can you do about it? You can do something about it!!

The plan you've created is not meant to be put up on the shelf. This is a working document. You made some commitments and set the intention to grow and achieve the success as you've defined it.

Continue to enjoy your journey!! The next chapter of Self-Discovery is Purposeful Connections!! You're not on an island. You need others and others need you!

NOTES

_____
_____
_____
_____
_____
_____
_____
_____
_____
_____
_____
_____
_____
_____
_____
_____
_____
_____
_____
_____

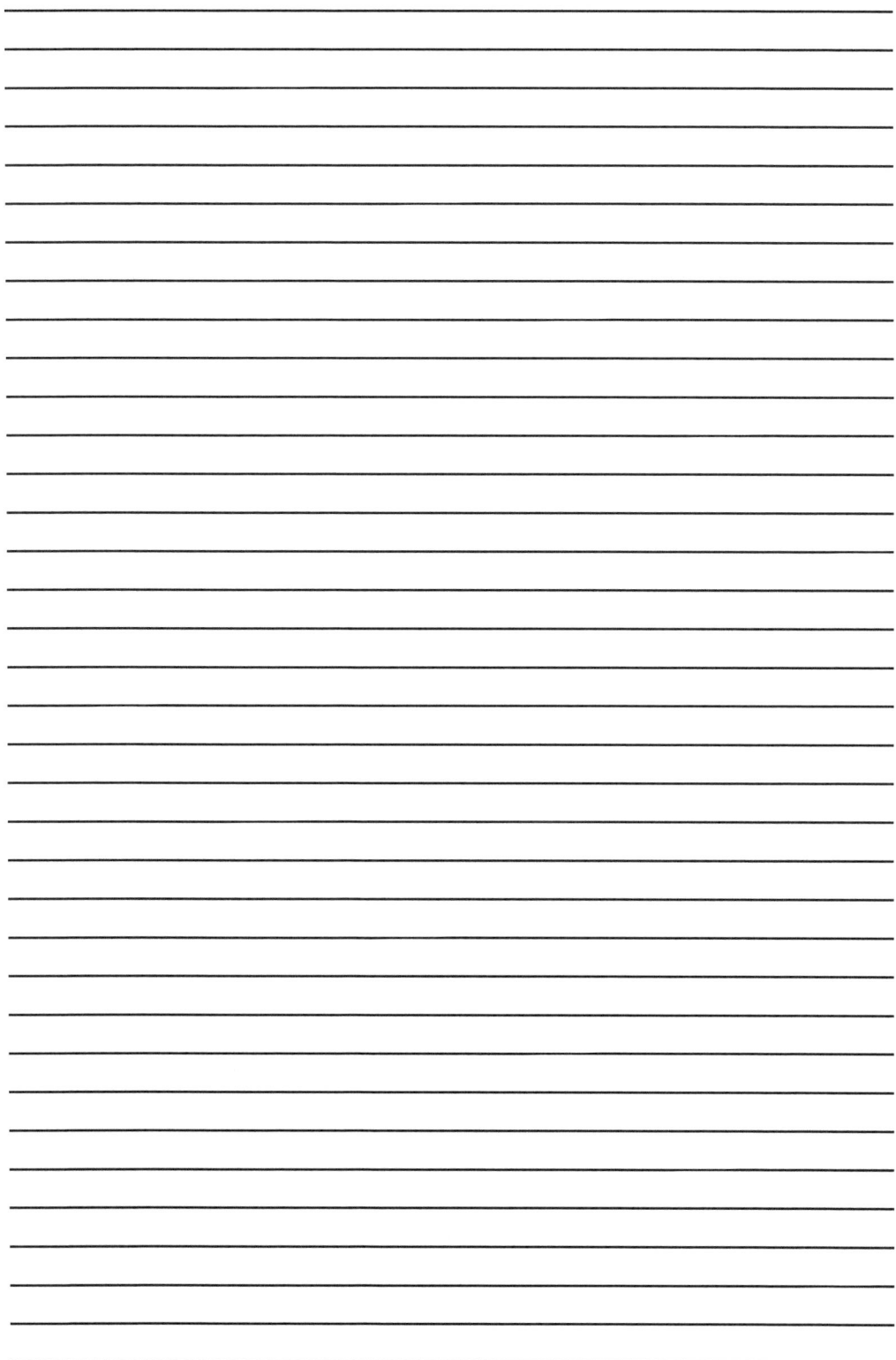

Chapter 3: Connecting with Purpose

Now that you have completed your strategic plan (Clarity statement, vision, and goals) and understood how to optimize your time, you must with purpose identify and connect with the resources you will need to help you achieve the success you desire. It is important to note that you cannot be successful working alone or on an island. It takes a village, and the resources are a part of your village. If you want more effective and efficient ways of achieving success, you must have a means to connect key resources into a single system better aligning with your mission, vision, goals, and outcomes. Developing a resource mapping strategy will facilitate your need to identify, align, and leverage the village resources to improve your chances of sustained success and growth. Mapping focuses on identifying assets and resources along with what they have to offer you to achieve your goals. Don't only think about local resources. With the advances in technology, you can leverage resources locally, regionally, and globally?

There are multiple benefits of going through a resource mapping exercise.
- Development of a more results-oriented system
- Gain in-depth information about the resources to leverage to meet your goals
- Identify challenges and opportunities to meet your specific needs
- Reflection on the value of existing resources while identifying new ones to optimize results
- Better alignment and coordination of resources
- Enhanced coordination and collaboration among relevant stakeholders
- Development of new strategies to better meet your goals and objectives.

Resource mapping principles and benefits
Through the mapping process, you must identify key stakeholders with expertise based on your life, business, and career. You want to ensure you recruit with the understanding of the role you want them to play, engage partners involving top level people and getting organized, and sustain by making their engagement meaningful, recognize contributions, and leadership rotation. You must also put strategies in place to keep stakeholders engaged.

Some examples of potential stakeholders are:
> **Life:** parents/family, friends, agency resources
> **Business:** business coach, business owners, suppliers, clients

Career: career coach, direct manager, sponsor, mentor

Your mapping principles will focus on:

- What is already present and available to build on its current strengths;
- Relationships are driven by the development of partnerships with a common interest in your success over a sustained period to accomplish your goals.
- What the resources have to offer that aligns with your goals
- Embracing the notion that to realize vision and meet goals resources may have to work across boundaries
- Addressing goals across your key life areas and the lack of resources required

It is critical throughout your journey that you meet on a regular basis to discuss progress and any requirements to adapt.

Your exercise for this module is to complete the Resource Optimization Map where you will identify the key resources/stakeholders and assets required to ensure your success. Remember it takes a village! You will gather the Stakeholder information below for your Resource Optimization Map:

- Company and contact name, address, phone number, email, and website
- Impact, influence, and contributions the stakeholder has on your achievement
- Self-interest of stakeholders (connecting is also about helping others)
- Steps to connect with your stakeholder
- Resource overlaps and duplications, gaps and missing resources, and the implications that
  impede success
- Technical assistance, tools, and finances needed - Who will source and how much?

THE LAW OF YOUR INNER CIRCLE

Those closest to you as a leader will determine your potential. No one ever does anything great alone! You must be strategic in creating your inner circle by ensuring they:

1) Have high influence with others
2) Bring a complimentary gift to the table
3) Hold a strategic position in your life, business, or career
4) Add value to your success
5) Positively impact other inner circle members, and
6) Are competent, have character, and the right chemistry

Is everyone around you on a journey of growth? If not reconsider your relationships and make a change. You also need to be in someone's inner circle. Remember you GIVE to GET!!

Now it's time to think through to achieve the success as you define it, who you need and why, how will connections be made and leveraged, and what do the stakeholder need/want from you (be sure you can deliver). Leverage the online template on ignitewithin.org. Use it as you reflect, and research on this exercise as a means to document resource

Resource Optimization Map (example)

Company Name	Contact Name	Inner Circle note "Yes" as appropriate	Phone	Email	Address

overlaps, gaps, missing resources, implications, technical assistance and tools required, and your financial requirements (this does not take the place of a budget). Or you can create your own but ensure it captures these critical points. Resource mapping is a critical step toward your success. Make this a living document – don't put it on the shelf. As you are creating your Resource Map exercise place a "yes" in the Inner Circle column as a reminder that those resources are the closest to you in helping you achieve the success you desire.

Website	Impact on Your Achievement (high, med, low)	Influence over Project Goal (high, med, low)	Stakeholder Self-Interest	Stakeholder Contribution	Steps to Connect with Stakeholder

Now that you understand how to optimize new and existing resources let's turn to ensuring you are connecting with a purpose in an influential way. It's not automatic. It takes knowing how and practicing. As a certified international John Maxwell coach, speaker, and teacher, I learned his five principles and practices to help you understand how not to connect and not just communicate. I am talking about connecting that increases your influence with your clients, family, friends, co-workers, bosses, suppliers, and other supporters. It gets you closer to what you want – job, business opportunity, marriage, and right family relationships. I encourage you to purchase the book, Everybody Communicates Few Connect on Amazon.com, to understand these principles and practices in more depth. Connecting is the only way to lead to your success. I've said it before – you are not on an island. You need others, and they need you. I have highlighted John Maxwell's connection philosophy below:

Connecting Principles:
1. Connecting increases your influence in every situation: Make your words count
2. Connecting is all about others – Give to get
3. Connecting goes beyond words – Body language, tone, energy
4. Connecting always requires energy – Got to do the work, network
5. Connecting is more skill than natural talent – Study and practice, value content

Connecting Practices:
1. Connectors connect on common ground
2. Connectors keep it simple
3. Connectors create an experience everyone enjoys
4. Connectors inspire people
5. Connectors live what they communicate

Words of great wisdom from John.

Take the steps below to start your journey to connect and not just communicate.
Identify three ways you can improve your ability to connect with one action to take make it happen. For me, I now listen to learn more about the other person, challenge my fears of approaching new people, and be authentic.

1 _____
2 _____
3 _____

What habits will you deploy to ensure you bring value to others? I work to operate from compassion, study my craft to understand problems identifying potential solutions, and listen.

_____

_____

_____

_____

_____

Get feedback from others to understanding your strengths and weaknesses when connecting with them. Don't take anything personal. It is all to help you. Jot down below some feedback noting how you can improve and being thankful for the honest feedback regardless of what it is.

_____

_____

_____

_____

_____

Reflect to ensure you are not operating out of arrogance and indifference. Are you asking open ending questions, and showing compassion and humility?

Note below some ways you can gain more common ground with those you must interact with (significant others, boss, employee, co-worker, family, friends). Once identified take action – try it!!

_____

_____

_____

_____

_____

_____

_____

_____

_____

_____

Congratulations on your willingness to do the work to grow and to ensure influential and purposeful connections!! You know growth is not automatic! The next chapter will be Communicating your Brand. Our approach is to learn not only to communicate but connect. Everyone communicates but few connect. How's your confidence? Any anxieties? Continue to be aware of how you are feeling as you are going through your journey of Self-Discovery.

NOTES

Chapter 4: Communicate Your Brand Locally, Regionally, Globally

Now that you know who you are through your Clarity Statement, the creation of your plan of action, and your connections, it is now time to reflect and determine how to communicate who you are – your brand! What separates you from everyone else locally/regionally/globally? How do you want to be perceived by others? How do you want to live your personal and business life? Remember, we are in a globally competitive environment in all aspects of our lives.

When communicating your brand do the below:
- Be authentic about your brand, transparent and open
- Show your personality – put a face to your brand
- Provide relevant content – it must be helpful by bringing value, solving problems, with quality engagements versus the number of engagements
- Communicate on non-brand topics – other industries, news, fun topics
- Create a means for your audience to contribute content and share -

What is a brand? It's a symbol, design, name, sound, reputation, emotion, employees, or tone that separates you from another individual or business. Your brand is an opportunity creator. Your brand creates recognition of your uniqueness and why you! Communicating your brand first begins by integrating your vision of your personal brand with understanding, developing, and prioritizing your communication goals that must align. You will not reach your desired results – success as you defined success – without effectively communicating to your target audience (stakeholders) – those who are critical in helping you achieve success. Avoid being overly optimistic especially in the initial phase, detailing obstacles, with plans to mitigate the risks. Involve others to gain their perspectives if they are an integral part of it or will be impacted by the results.

- You are unique! The Clarity Statement you created represents who you say you are – your brand. It has your gifts (bring out potential in others) and how you will use them (give guidance and direction) to impact others (women and girls), align your values (integrity), and achieve your personal outcomes (be valued, security, loved). When communicating my brand it aligns.

Let's now go through who to talk to, what messaging, and how and where to communicate your brand.

WHO is your Target Audience?

Every individual or business needs a target audience if you are selling or getting something – potential employer, client, friends, etc. You want to build a demographic community of people who will be an asset in helping you achieve your goals. Who is your target audience or in other words, who will pay or give, influence those people, and support you to ensure your success? It's a hobby if you're only doing this for yourself. My granddaughter who is two has a target audience – father, mother, grandmother. She knows that we can give her what she wants. She wants a cookie. She targets her father who says not today. She then targets her mother who says not today. She then targets me and most times I will give it to her. She now will come to me first to ask because she's learned that her best return is with grandma. I am sure you've done this or know of it happening. Same concept.

Based on your clarity statement, who did you say you wanted to impact based on using your gifts for your highest purpose? For my business, I am using my gifts for the purpose of bringing out the potential in others with an impact on women and girls. As a result, the audience I target are millennials in the workplace, working women over 40 making or wanting to make a transformative transition in their life, business, or career, and girls in high school. I target individuals and as well as companies who employ my target audience. I am targeting people who work and medium sized organizations who can pay, who can influence someone else, or a supporter who will spread the word.

I have counseled that I need to narrow my target audience to say millennials only. But I am choosing to do what I believe I am called to do. And my value proposition crosses over to multiple audiences – non-fear based transitions, leadership strategies, self-discovery. Remember you have to do what you deem is best for you but the broader your audience, the less focused you will be. Listen to others, but the decision is yours.

Determine the demographics of your target audience. I am choosing or example 40+ women because from my experience and talking with other women, we can be at a cross-road having lived our lives for everyone else but ourselves. What about you?

Consider these demographics and add more as you reflect on this along with why you are choosing the particular demographic.

Gender: _____   Country: _____   Religion: _____

Ethnicity: _____   Age Group: _____   Education: _____

Location: _____   Titles: _____   Income: $ _____

Biz Size: Revenue _____   Profits: _____   # employees _____

Why did you select the above demographic characteristics for what you want to achieve?

_____

_____

_____

_____

_____

_____

_____

WHAT message will you deliver to your target audience?

It is important to understand that the message you give is not only about what you can do for your target audience but messaging about you. Communication about your background, experiences, values, accomplishments, etc. will help your audience get to know you. Understanding what motivates your target audience and what problem they need to be solved. It's the only way you can ensure they know you well enough to allow you to develop solutions that will help them achieve their goals or solve the problem while also achieving your goals – You Get What You Give! Take the time to understand and have empathy with your audience. Is your audience motivated by career/business growth, cost savings, productivity, work/life balance, financial security, be of value, etc. Your message is about building a relationship with your audience to demonstrate you have their best interests in mind.

My messaging journey resulted in helping women and girls discover or rediscover who they are and want to be and ensuring a plan of action according to success as they defined it. Hence, this book as a guide to self-discovery. I talked to many women in the US, Nigeria, Ghana, and Kenya and found this to be a common concern. They were not satisfied with their current situation, afraid to make a move, didn't know how to make a successful move, or didn't make themselves a priority to focus on ensuring transformation. You get my point! You are taking the right step and putting you first to get what you want – the rest will follow.

Take a few moments to think about your target audience, talk to a few people, and then write down some key messages you want to ensure are delivered to your audience. Let me also encourage you to consider getting help as appropriate as this is key to your success. Know your lane and strengths and get right resources to support and offset your weaknesses. I've hired someone to help me with messaging. I understand the motivations and problems for my audience but needed help optimizing the message.

Ensure your messaging is creative, memorable, and consistent.

_____
_____
_____
_____
_____
_____

WHERE is the audience you're working to reach?

Working and living in Nigeria for a few years, allowed me to understand the importance of having a local/regional/global perspective on my marketability in the workforce and now as a business owner. With the advances in technology, one can have a world market, i.e., online store, leveraging social media, Skype for video communications. I've leveraged Skype for coaching clients in Nigeria. It all depends on what you want and what you are ready to do. You can begin locally with a regional or global direction in the future. Even when considering local, what does that mean city, county, state? Start by thinking where your existing circle is and expand from there. You can research various online locations to determine if there is a market for your products or services, i.e., Google, Department of Commerce, Chambers of Commerce (state, city, county), and Small Business Administration. They are all very helpful in all areas of business.

Ensure you are networking in the regions where you want to do business and support the community. Note below your target areas and research the resources that can help you understand the needs of those sectors that align with your services and products.

_____
_____
_____
_____

HOW will you communicate your brand message and its frequency?

There are so many ways to communicate your brand message. Let's start with how you need to be communicating your brand. Then we will discuss various vehicles of communication like social media, websites, etc.

How Are You Communicating Personally YOU

You cannot be effective in communicating your brand if you are not confident in knowing who you are. It just won't happen. You have to leave someone with a feeling of confidence that you know you, are credible, have values, and personable or relatable. Many times you are in front of people – you must be by the way. Tweet, texts, emails are alright, but you have to be in front of individuals. When you meet someone for the first time, how do you communicate who you are? I've met people, and the first thing could be a handshake. Is it a firm shake or limp? Limp doesn't reflect confidence.

When you introduce yourself do you read off your business card – name, company, what you do?. That's it!! Or do you engage with others? Hi, I am Gladys Agwai, Founder, and CEO of Ignite Within and we move our clients away from their fears to live and work in their highest purpose and passion. How are you today? What a great event! Are you a part of the organization? What do you do? Where do you live? Family? What do you like about what you do? What's your next move? You get the point. Engage in conversation. Find something in common or discuss something memorable. I will always fit in living and working in Africa as a differentiator and how my life changed. What's something different about you that you can make memorable to that individual? You want them to remember you six months from then in case they meet someone who may be able to help you. I've had that happen and got a call wanting me to meet someone interested in doing business in Nigeria or had a connection they wanted me to meet who was interested in coaching. You want strategic relationships.

Think about whether in your life, business, or career the percentage of your time spent on performance, exposure, and image, work versus family or recreation. Life balance is imperative to your health, well-being, and growth. Women spend 80% of their time on performance with little time getting exposure and focusing on their image. Men do the opposite (not that they don't perform). Get out and get the exposure you need to build your brand, set the right image, and establish and build relationships.

Take some time to reflect on how you are currently positioning yourself when in front of others and what are you doing well and what can you improve?

_____

_____

_____

_____

_____

_____

_____

Vehicles to Communicate Your Brand

In today's globally competitive environment, it is critical that the media you select to communicate your brand has a local, regional, and global influence. With the advances of technology, we can do business, meet significant others, friends, participate in associations and networking activities from anywhere. My target audience is both in US and Africa with focus on Nigeria, Ghana, and Kenya. As a result, the mediums that I choose must reach those areas and must include online communication vehicles as well as face-to-face and print mediums. For my coaching clients in Nigeria, I use Skype. Social media will provide that global reach to your audience as appropriate.

Some of the key tools available for personal and business accounts are noted below. Check which ones you will leverage and why. Don't forget that social media groups can be a valuable place to promote your brand, network, and learn.

ALL MESSAGING TYPES

LinkedIn: _____

Facebook: _____

Twitter: _____

Email: _____

Website: _____

Blog: _____

Press Release: _____

TV: _____

IMAGE MESSAGING

Instagram: _____

Pinterest: _____

SnapChat: _____

AUDIO/VIDEO MESSAGING
YouTube: _____

Sound Cloud: _____

Facebook Live: _____

BOOK
Book: _____

eBook: _____

Audio Book: _____

You can also leverage and expand your brand messaging through interviews on audio and video podcasts, TV, and streaming TV that is positioned on iTunes, Roku, and other streaming solutions. That just happened based on networking I had done attending a conference and a meeting with a friend on his new business venture. I wasn't meeting to seek participation on a podcast or TV. Their connection happened to be involved in this and once known to me I "asked" if I could participate. This allowed me to communicate my brand in a unique way and leverage it to repurpose it on social media. I've also been asked to host my on TV program which would further expand my brand message. But you have to be ready to take on the task if you accept. Press releases can also be valuable in announcing something pertinent about you or your business or an activity where you're involved.

When selecting the vehicle to use, consider your target audience. LinkedIn is for professional/business communication and thought leadership. The messaging on LinkedIn will be different than the messaging to use for example Snap Chat which is used by millennials and younger, and the picture messaging goes away after 24 hours. Also, consider what groups are in each medium and which ones cater to your target audience. Determine which medium is used by your target audience.

You must be purposeful and intentional no matter who and where the target audience, what messages to communicate, and how you will communicate and its frequency. Wrong choices will hurt your brand, take your money, and waste your time (although there will be learning lessons).

Other key factors to consider when communicating your brand are:
1. The resources or budget that you will use to support your communications strategy, including projections for future costs. You will need to invest time and money.
2. Provide a timeline for the implementation and the frequency of communication
3. Evaluating the success of your communications through surveys, social media **metrics, new relationships, new business opportunity meetings, new job or sales.**
4. **Conditions change, you must adapt and respond.**

NOTES

Chapter 5: Capitalize on Opportunities

I applaud you for reaching this point in your journey to self-discovery! You have clarity of purpose, created your strategic plan challenging your fears, ensured purposeful connections through resource mapping, and understand how to communicate your brand globally. This last chapter will help you to capitalize better on opportunities within your scope.

To capitalize on anything means, you are willing to take a chance to gain something, to get an advantage, profit from, make the most of, or exploit a situation. You want to capitalize on opportunity using the highest level of integrity. Why? One word Karma!! You reap what you sew. There is enough in the universe for everyone. No need to be underhanded about how you capitalize or seize opportunities. I know people in life, business and corporate who are willing to do anything to get what they want. No integrity! You don't want any part of that, and it can offset anything you've gained if you set the wrong intention and then act on it.

BE MINDFUL

Most people miss opportunities that are right in front of them because they aren't looking for them. Opportunities present themselves to us. Are you even aware when an opportunity comes your way? Or are they passing you by leaving you wondering why you are not experiencing the progress and success you want? In chapter one, we discussed being mindful. For you to capitalize on the opportunity, you must be "aware" of what an opportunity looks like, pay "attention" to it, set an intention to do something about it, and then act to make it happen. Walk through your life journey moment to moment being mindful of your internal and external experiences.

Keep your eyes wide open and grab those opportunities as they come your way even those that appear ugly. Anyone that you see as a success has kept their eyes open.

CAPTURED BY FEAR!

Another area we discussed in Chapter one was about your mind viruses. The negative thinking that impacts you and others. Those that will hold you back or propel you forward. Opportunities come our way, but we can't capitalize out of fear. Remember the five beliefs we discussed: 1) self-worth, 2) capability, 3) readiness, 4) desire, and 5) am I good enough. Even if you recognize an opportunity, you will let it go because of the beliefs I mentioned. And if you allow fear capture you, you will not capitalize on any opportunities impeding your success and the success of others. You bring others along when you grow. Go back and reflect on mind viruses that came up for you when you realized you missed an opportunity. Don't just let it go. Reflect, understand and find the permanent cure to manage your mind viruses.

WHAT'S THE PROBLEM?

We face problems every day. Within those problems, there is an opportunity. You have to be solutions oriented versus continually focusing on the problem. What are some problems with your clients, suppliers, or relationships? What can you do to help – provide a service, product, advice, information, or change behavior to improve the relationship? As I was having conversations with women and girls, I found a common problem. They were afraid and felt powerless to change the situation. My program solves that problem by giving them their power back and helping them to challenge their fears. Be mindful of the problems around you and be solutions oriented. Got a solution to a problem? Capitalize on it.

IGNITE THAT GUT FEELING

Throughout my life, I have gone through many transitions. When in corporate, I transitioned through different organizations and levels, from the US to Africa, to retirement and my own business. At each transition, I had to sit with myself and go within before, during, and after the transition. Have you ever had a gut feeling that stayed with you? Something was igniting within you to make a change. When thinking about the programs for my business, my gut kept reminding me of the transitions I've made, my fears, transformation, and success. I took what I faced and used it as an opportunity to create a solution that would benefit others who go through transitions which all have degrees of fear within us. It is one of my most important programs that I offer and one needed as I have had conversations with individuals and businesses. What's your gut telling you? Sit with it and think through how you can create an opportunity and capitalize on it. More than likely other people are experiencing the same thing and looking for your unique solution.

GET OUT OF THE BOX

I know you've heard the phrase "out of the box thinking." I've always wondered why we are in the box in the first place. Get out of the box and begin to look further than the walls of your box. Look ahead to see what other people want or will want. Steve Jobs, CEO Apple, set the example of getting out of the box. Bill Gates another. Oprah Winfrey who is my hero! They all are mindful, challenge their fears, see not just the problems but the opportunities and solutions of today and the future, and then make it happen. Their lives were dedicated from the beginning to be outside of the box which brought growth for them and others.

LISTEN PLEASE!

Do you talk too much? When I was in sales, we were taught to listen and let the client talk. Listening will give insight into what others are saying and feeling. Do you notice when you are in a room those who observe and listen versus talk, talk, talk? The ones who listen are usually the smartest people in the room. They get it. It's about other people not just you getting your point across or feeding your ego. Yes, I said it! You won't notice an opportunity has come up when you can't hear, and you respond versus listen. Seek out successful people who are within your areas of interest and listen.

COPY CAT WITH AN EDGE!

Don't be discouraged by your competition. You are unique and can do it with an edge. I leverage my global edge within my business based on my global corporate experience and clients. It is impactful both in the US and Africa conversations. As they say, nothing is new under the sun. You must differentiate and be innovative with what already exists.

KEEP IT SIMPLE

What complicates your world or the world of others? Complications lead to pain points that need solutions. Living and working in Nigeria put me up close and personal with difficulties that we take for granted in the US. Most transactions are complicated, multi-step, and paper driven for consumers. It was frustrating coming from the US with its technology advances. My role as a sales executive was to work with helping my clients help ease the pain of their end users through technology. Hootsuite is a marketing tool that made life simple for business owners who leveraged social media. It allows one to load their messaging and schedule it across the social media platforms. Before it had to be done separately. The old cell phones when texting had to hit the button three times to get to the letter C. A simple solution to update the keyboard.

REPLICATE SUCCESS

Money is not the root of all evil. It is great as long as you keep it in perspective. Remember it's about intention. Rather than spending too much time on the smaller opportunities, you can focus on those that give you a higher return on your energy and time spent. Who are your key clients, companies, or relationships with the potential to give you the most of what you want - revenue or income or satisfaction? Tap into where the action is and listen out for the unmet need those pain points. Focus on those who are successful. Review where you or others have been successful and replicate the success.

I have noted nine ways to capitalize on opportunity will get you focused on making wisdom choices to optimize and succeed. Use the next page to note where your areas of opportunity are and how you can capitalize on them.

NOTES

In Conclusion!

You now know the importance and how to come out from under that shade to shine your light on who you are authentically. Or as Michelle Obama said "Live Out Loud." You matter and the world needs you and what you have to give.

It is your choice, no one else's to live your life according to the plan God has for you and who you were created to be. Don't be fearful of getting to know you! It is the most important work you will ever do. And it is not selfish at all. It's actually more selfish if you don't do this work to finally focus on you. You will be amazed at what you will attract once you are confident in the real you. Imposter no more – no more pretending – no more fake interactions. Be liberated knowing that you are enough!

Do the work! Don't be Scared!! Play to Win!

ADDITIONAL NOTES

Clarity/Mission Statement: _____

_____

Vision Statement: _____

_____

Three Focused Life Areas: 1) _____ 2) _____ 3) _____

Play to Win Goals

Key Life Area	GOAL (Start with 5 Key Goals)	Completion Date	Tasks Required to Complete Goal	ROE (Return on Energy) Yes or No?

Five Key Goals from Overall Work Completed:

1) _____
2) _____
3) _____
4) _____
5) _____

Completion Date	Obstacles	Skill Gaps	Resources Needed	Opportunities Identified

www.ingramcontent.com/pod-product-compliance
Lightning Source LLC
Chambersburg PA
CBHW041105110426
42740CB00043B/154